Rabbit in the Well

by Catherine Baker

illustrated by Irina Avgustinovich

"I need food!" said Fox.
"Rabbit will be my dinner!"

Fox ran to get Rabbit.
Rabbit was quicker than Fox.

Rabbit ran to a well.
It was deep and dark.

Rabbit got into the bucket.

Then the bucket fell!
Rabbit fell, too.

Soon, Fox trotted to the well.

Rabbit was a quick thinker.
"I am fishing!" she said.

"The fish are good!" said Rabbit.
"Come down and see!"

"I love fish!" said Fox.
"I will pull up the bucket."

Rabbit was out.
Fox got in.

The bucket fell down the well.
So did Fox!

Soon, Fox was howling.

"There are no fish in this well!" he said.

"No," said Rabbit.
"But there is a fox in it!"

"Just you wait!" said Fox.
"I will get you!"

Now, Rabbit had run far off.

Encourage students to look at the pictures and talk about Fox's feelings in each one.